FANTASTIC FAILS

Learning from Bad Ideas

TRANSPORTATION BREAKDOWNS

BY AMIE JANE LEAVITT

CAPSTONE PRESS
a capstone imprint

Capstone Captivate is published by Capstone Press,
an imprint of Capstone.
1710 Roe Crest Drive
North Mankato, Minnesota 56003
www.capstonepub.com

Copyright © 2020 by Capstone. All rights reserved.
No part of this publication may be reproduced in whole or in part, or stored in a retrieval system, or transmitted in any form or by any means, electronic, mechanical, photocopying, recording, or otherwise, without written permission of the publisher.

Library of Congress Cataloging-in-Publication Data is available on the Library of Congress website.
ISBN: 978-1-5435-9212-2 (library binding)
ISBN: 978-1-4966-6621-5 (paperback)
ISBN: 978-1-5435-9216-0 (eBook PDF)

Summary: See some of the world's fastest transportation breakdowns at lightning speed. Find out how each form of transportation failed, the basic engineering missed during construction, and what engineers learned from their mistakes.

Image Credits
Alamy: Sueddeutsche Zeitung Photo, 38; Getty Images: Bettmann, 34, Hulton Archive, 25; Library of Congress: 14, 44 (top); The New York Public Library: 5; Newscom: dpa/picture-alliance/Frank M Chler, 37, Heritage Images/Index Fototeca, 26, Imagine China, 41, Reuters/Stephen Hird, 30, SIPA/Chine Nouvelle, 42, Universal Images Group/Dorling Kindersley, 18, World History Archive, 9, 12; Shutterstock: blambca, cover (illustration), Everett Historical, 13, 22, John Selway, 29, pisaphotography, 6, PNIK, cover (background), Steve Lagreca, 33 (bottom); SuperStock: Science and Society/Past Pix, 21; Wikimedia: Doug Duncan, 33 (top), Public Domain, 10, 17, 44 (bottom), 45 (all), Timmymiller, 23

Design Elements: Shutterstock

Editorial Credits
Editor: Mari Bolte; Designer: Jennifer Bergstrom; Media Researcher: Eric Gohl; Production Specialist: Laura Manthe

All internet sites appearing in back matter were available and accurate when this book was sent to press.

Printed and bound in the United States of America.
PA100

TABLE OF CONTENTS

CHAPTER

1 PUSH AND PULL
BEACH'S PNEUMATIC TRANSIT SYSTEM 4

2 WHOOSH!
THE MOVING SIDEWALK 8

3 LIFTOFF!
SAMUEL LANGLEY'S AERODROME 12

4 THE UNSINKABLE SINKER
THE *TITANIC* 16

5 BIG BALLOONS:
THE ZEPPELIN 20

6 FLOATING ON AIR
THE AÉROTRAIN 24

7 JET-SETTER
THE CONCORDE 28

8 LEMON IN THE SKY
THE FLYING PINTO 32

9 BEEP BEEP
DICKMANNS'S SELF-DRIVING CAR 36

10 WATCH YOUR HEAD!
TRANSIT ELEVATED BUS 40

DRIVING, FLYING, AND LAUNCHING THROUGH HISTORY 44
GLOSSARY 46
READ MORE 47
INTERNET SITES 47
INDEX 48

Words in **bold** are in the glossary.

WHETHER WE WALK, RIDE, BIKE, OR FLY, we expect to travel safely. But sometimes inventions designed to get us from here to there go wrong. Sometimes the ideas never even get off the ground! No matter what the failure, though, there's always something we can learn afterward.

CHAPTER 1
PUSH AND PULL
BEACH'S PNEUMATIC TRANSIT SYSTEM

Construction on New York City's **Pneumatic** Transit System began in 1869. Developed by inventor Alfred Ely Beach, it was the first attempt to build an underground public transportation network in the city.

A pneumatic system moves objects by air pressure. A huge fan created enough wind to push the train forward in the tube from station A to station B. When the train needed to return to station A, the fan's direction was reversed so the wind went the opposite way. The suction created in the tube pulled the train back to the starting point.

Beach was so sure his pneumatic transit system would work that he contributed $350,000 of his own money to the project. That's nearly $7 million today.

Air Delivery

Pneumatic systems can be found in everyday uses. At drive-up banks, customers place money in a little canister. With the push of a button, the canister is sucked up a tube and delivered to the teller inside the bank. Similar systems are used in hospitals, offices, libraries, factories, airports, and post offices. One restaurant in New Zealand installed pipes to deliver burgers and fries straight from the kitchen.

FACT: Alfred Ely Beach was the main editor of the magazine *Scientific American*, which is still in print today.

A Modern Subway

Beach's first subway system paved the way for later underground railways. New York City wouldn't be the same without its underground transportation network. Today more than 800 miles (1,285 kilometers) of subway track get more than 5.5 million riders where they need to be every day.

GRAND OPENING!

The tunnel ran underneath the city's famous theater district, Broadway. It stretched from Murray Street to Warren Street. The train was rounded to fit inside the tunnel. As many as 22 passengers could ride in the train at a time.

Construction on the underground subway system in New York City started in 1900. It opened to passengers in 1904.

The train's grand opening was on February 26, 1870. Over the next year, about 400,000 people hopped on board. Many did so just for the fun of it, because it was a short ride. From end to end, the 312-foot (95-meter)-long tunnel only stretched about one city block. It was never able to expand to offer a longer journey.

FACT: Pneumatics may not be used to move entire trains today, but they are used in the train's moving parts. Train doors open and close through a system of pressurized air. Some train brakes use air pressure too.

Lessons Learned

Beach's idea wasn't a terrible one, and it did work. However, an aboveground train system was built in New York at about the same time. It quickly became the main form of mass transport in the city. In comparison, Beach's underground network was nothing but a **novelty**. He tried to get permission to continue his tunnel all the way to Central Park but was denied his request. The project, which would cost $1 million per mile of tunnel, was too expensive. Sometimes a project fails because it's just not practical.

CHAPTER 2
WHOOSH!
THE MOVING SIDEWALK

What if you could get from here to there at your own pace? Inventor Alfred Speer dreamed of moving sidewalks that would transport passengers at different speeds. He received a patent for his idea in 1871.

HOW IT WORKED

The first moving sidewalk was built for Chicago's World's Fair in 1893. It ran along the 3,300-foot (1,006-m)-long Navy **Pier** and brought visitors from steamboats landing on the pier to the city's fairgrounds.

There were two sets of sidewalks that ran parallel to each other. One moved at 2 to 3 miles (3.2 to 4.8 km) an hour. The other one sped along at

FACT: Another famous invention introduced at the Chicago World's Fair of 1893 was the Ferris wheel.

The moving sidewalk had space for people to stand or sit.

twice the speed. The faster-moving sidewalk even had benches for riders to relax on as they journeyed to the fair. Generally, people started out on the slower-moving sidewalk, adjusted to the movement, and then changed lanes.

Chicago's World's Fair was also known as the World's Columbian Exposition. The fair covered 600 acres (243 hectares).

NOT-SO-SMOOTH RIDE

The sidewalk ran in a loop so people could hitch a ride going both ways. It could carry 6,000 people at a time. Around 31,000 people rode the sidewalk every hour, at a cost of 5 cents a ride.

Unfortunately, the sidewalk wasn't a flawless machine. It had some mechanical issues and would often break down mid-ride. This was frustrating for both the riders and the operators. Construction delays also meant that the sidewalk wasn't ready until closer to the end of the fair.

Speer never had a chance to completely figure out the flaws in his system. Buildings on the pier caught fire the next year. The moving sidewalk was lost in the blaze.

Speer Moves Forward

Speer and his business partners continued to improve upon their original plans. A later idea included a walkway with three **elevated** platforms. The fastest one would move along at 19 miles (31 km) per hour. It would have enclosed cars where people could sit and relax.

They suggested ideas for moving sidewalks in major cities throughout the United States. City planners rejected each proposal, though. They were concerned that the systems wouldn't be reliable in bad weather and might break down too easily.

Lessons Learned

Speer had other ideas for moving sidewalks, including one that ran along New York City's Broadway for theatergoers and one that crossed the Brooklyn Bridge. **Skeptics** wondered how they would hold up in bad weather. Who would fix them? And how were they better than a bus or streetcar?

Speer's idea wasn't completely rejected. Today moving walkways can be found at airports, train stations, and amusement parks. However, these are really very simplified versions of what the original inventors of the moving walkways had in mind.

CHAPTER 3
LIFTOFF!

SAMUEL LANGLEY'S AERODROME

At the beginning of the 1900s, inventors competed to be the first to make a flying machine. In order to qualify as the first, it had to be heavier than air, powered by a machine, and carry a human.

Samuel Langley was one of those inventors. He was an **astronomer**. He also worked at the Smithsonian Museum and studied how and why things fly. Langley designed a machine called an aerodrome. He worked with models to perfect his ideas.

Langley started with small models around 12 feet (3.7 m) wide.

LANGLEY'S AERODROMES

Full-scale Aerodrome
Wingspan: 48 feet, 5 inches (15 m)
Length: 52 feet, 5 inches (16 m)
Height: 11 feet, 4 inches (3.5 m)
Weight: 750 pounds (340 kilograms), including pilot

Quarter-scale Aerodrome
Wingspan: 12 feet (3.7 m)
Length: 15 feet (4.7 m)
Height: 3 feet, 6 inches (1 m)
Weight: 42 pounds (19 kg)

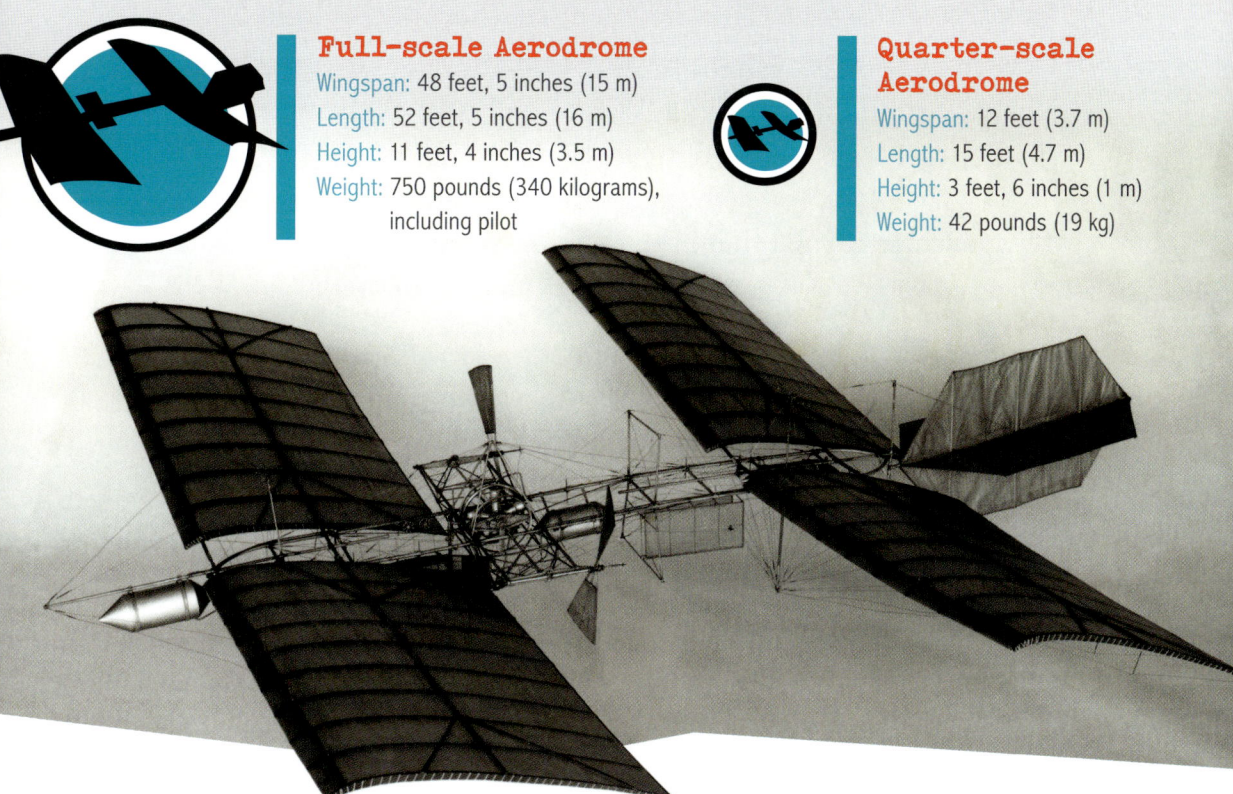

A catapult mounted to a boat propelled his double-winged aerodromes into the sky. Then a steam-powered, gasoline-fueled engine would send them through the air at about 30 miles (50 km) per hour.

The models were a success. In 1896, they took their first flights near the Potomac River in Virginia. They were still missing one thing, though: a human passenger. Langley knew that was his next step.

Wright Brothers Flight

The Wright brothers were other inventors competing in the race for a flying machine. They had their first successful flight on December 17, 1903. Their powered airplane flew at Kitty Hawk, North Carolina, with Orville Wright on board as the pilot. The flight lasted for 12 seconds. The plane traveled 120 feet (37 m).

Their success earned them the Langley Medal for **Aerodynamics**, which was awarded to them in 1909.

Langley's launch in October 1903

THE GREAT AERODROME

Langley was given a **grant** from the U.S. government for $50,000 to help him build his aircraft. His plan was to **scale** up his aerodrome models to fit a human inside. This didn't work. The engine wasn't powerful enough to lift both a plane and a person. But a bigger engine meant more weight.

Langley had a more powerful engine built. He changed up the design of the aircraft. Finally, he felt like he had something that would work. The finished aerodrome was nearly 50 feet (15 m) wide and 52 feet (16 m) long.

In October 1903, he tested his new aircraft without a passenger. It crashed into the river. He pulled it out and repaired it. Then he tried again on December 8. It crashed just like before. Langley blamed the launching equipment. He asked for additional funding, but was denied.

Nine days later, Orville and Wilbur Wright succeeded where Langley had failed.

Lessons Learned

Just because something works on a small scale doesn't mean it will work at full size. Think about a paper airplane. It may fly fine when it's made of notebook paper. But it probably wouldn't fly very well if it was built large enough to hold a human. Engineers must consider various factors, such as wingspan and weight, when they build their model to make sure that it will behave just like the real thing.

CHAPTER 4
THE UNSINKABLE SINKER

THE *TITANIC*

It was April 1912, and the RMS *Titanic* was ready to sail. Built using the best engineering knowledge of the time, it was the fastest—and safest—ship in the world. Some people said it was practically unsinkable.

Passengers and crew members felt invincible on the huge ship. The *Titanic*'s **hull** was constructed of thousands of steel plates that were 1 inch (2.5 centimeters) thick. The plates were connected with millions of rivets. The bottom of the ship had 16 special watertight compartments. If the hull was ever punctured, these sections could be closed off to keep water from entering the rest of the ship.

On April 10, 1912, the *Titanic* set sail. On April 14, the captain received at least six warnings that there were icebergs nearby. At 11:40 p.m., lookouts spied an enormous iceberg straight ahead. The crew tried to steer away from the huge 100-foot (31-m)-tall iceberg, but there wasn't enough time. The side of the *Titanic* struck the iceberg just 37 seconds later.

TITANIC BY THE NUMBERS

- **3,000**
the number of people who worked on building the ship

- **883 feet**
(269 m)
the length of the boat

- **3,547**
the ship's capacity, including passengers and crew

- **24 knots**
(28 miles per hour)
the ship's top speed

- **64**
the number of lifeboats needed to rescue every person on board

- **20**
the number of lifeboats actually on board

Hundreds of people, including some of the wealthiest in the world, bought tickets for *Titanic*'s maiden voyage.

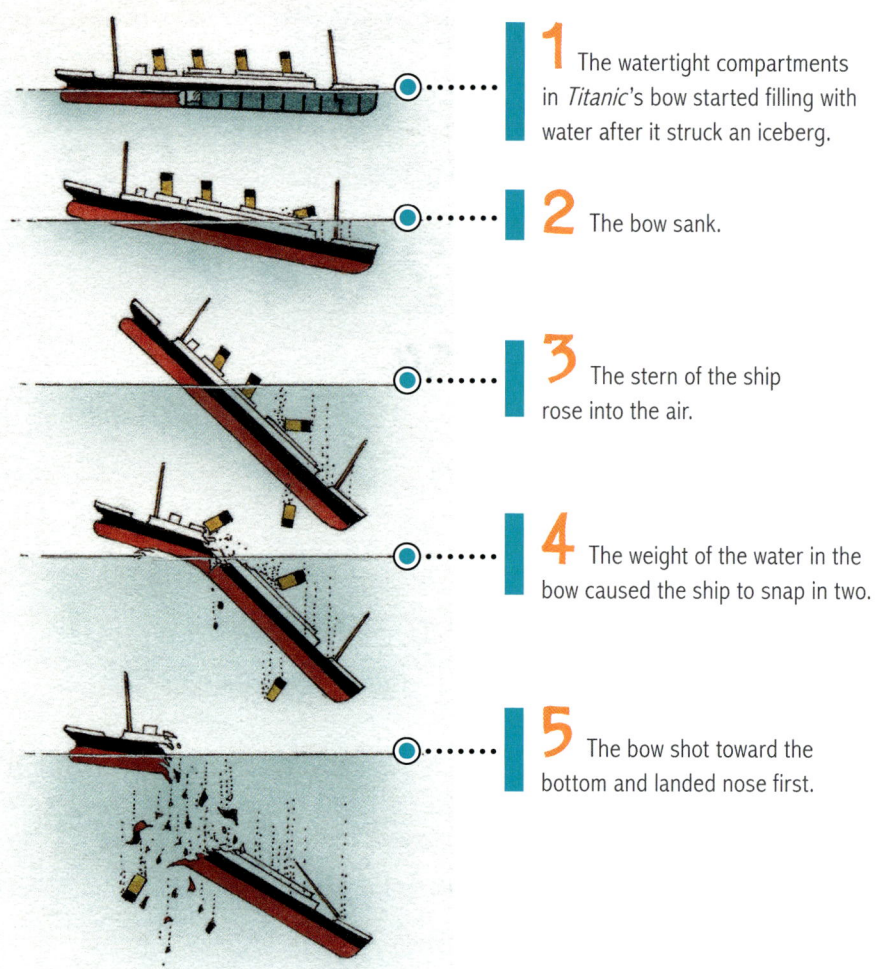

1 The watertight compartments in *Titanic*'s bow started filling with water after it struck an iceberg.

2 The bow sank.

3 The stern of the ship rose into the air.

4 The weight of the water in the bow caused the ship to snap in two.

5 The bow shot toward the bottom and landed nose first.

TRAGEDY AT SEA

Water began rushing in. It filled one compartment after another. The walls of the compartments were not tall enough to keep the water from spilling from one compartment to the next. The bow began to tilt downward. The more it tilted, the more water came in. The "unsinkable" ship was sinking.

The *Titanic* broke in two a little after 2:00 a.m. Both parts of the ship quickly sank to the bottom of the sea.

When officers knew the ship was sinking, they started loading lifeboats with women and children. Some of the passengers had been told not to worry and go back to bed. Others were told to get onto the lifeboats. There were not enough lifeboats for everyone on board. Those who did not make it onto the lifeboats died. According to the U.S. Senate committee that oversaw a hearing about the accident, 1,517 people died in the disaster.

LEARNING FROM TRAGEDY

Problem	Lesson Learned
People believed the *Titanic* couldn't sink	Nothing in life is 100 percent safe.
The crew ignored the warnings about the icebergs.	People should always listen to warnings from others.
There weren't enough lifeboats on board.	Safety should always be a priority.
The watertight compartments had openings at the top of the walls, so they weren't really watertight. No one expected that water would rise that high in the ship.	Engineers need to look at their designs and ask questions like, "Will this still work even if the worst-case scenario happens?"
The *Titanic* had a single hull instead of a double hull.	Double hulls prevent water from entering the interior of the ship.

CHAPTER 5
BIG BALLOONS:
THE ZEPPELIN

THE RIGID AIRSHIP

The zeppelin was the world's first **rigid** airship. It was invented by German Count Ferdinand, Graf von Zeppelin, in 1900. It had a metal frame and was covered in big sheets of fabric called envelopes. It maintained its shape without any gas inside. However, in order to lift up into the sky, big bags inside had to be filled with hydrogen gas.

More improvements were made so the airships could carry passengers. In 1909, the *Graf Zeppelin* was first used to take people around Germany. By 1931, it was making regular flights between Germany and North and South America. The *Graf Zeppelin* made nearly 600 flights and crossed the Atlantic Ocean 144 times.

The *Graf Zeppelin* was powered by a propeller and a steam engine. It could travel about 80 miles (130 km) per hour and stay in the air for more than 100 hours.

Floating Along

Airships were used for many purposes. They were used during World War I (1914–1918). They transported passengers, carried mail, and aided the military. Advertisers paid to have their logos displayed along the sides of airships. Similar airships called blimps are still used today. Unlike zeppelins, blimps have no rigid skeletons. They are more like big balloons.

The crash of the *Hindenburg* was shared over the radio and recorded in photographs and on film. It was the first time audiences heard a tragedy in such audio and visual detail.

BUT THEN . . .

The *Graf Zeppelin's* success led to the building of other airships, including the *Hindenburg*. This new airship was bigger and could hold more passengers than the *Graf Zeppelin*.

The newer, more modern *Hindenburg* was supposed to be filled with helium instead of hydrogen. Helium is less **flammable** than hydrogen. But it was harder to find at the time, and in the end the ship was filled with hydrogen.

During the *Hindenburg's* second flight in 1937, the gas began to leak. The hydrogen mixed with oxygen, which created a flammable gas. An electric spark started a huge fire. The ship crashed, and 35 people died.

BIG, BIGGER, BIGGEST

The *Hindenburg* was 804 feet (245 m) in length and 135 feet (41 m) in diameter. It was more than three times larger than a Boeing 747 airplane and four times the size of the well-known Goodyear Blimp seen at many sporting events.

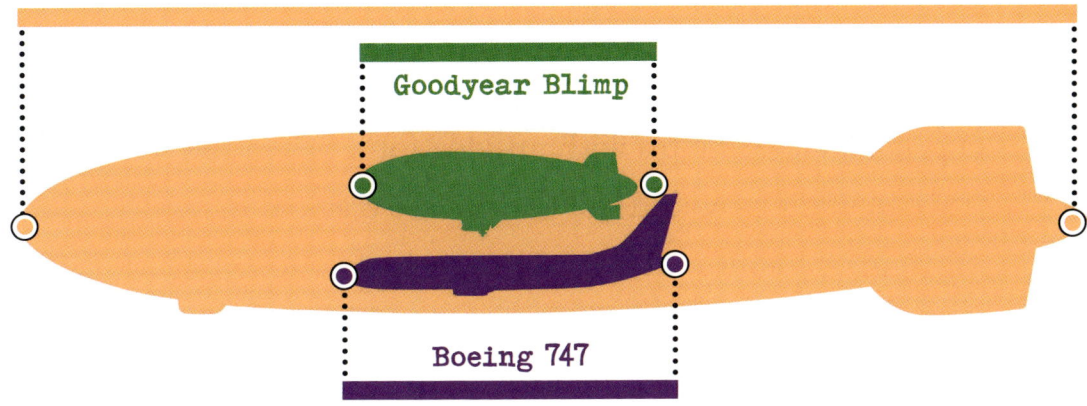

Lessons Learned

After the *Hindenburg* disaster, airships were never filled with hydrogen again in the United States. Today they are mainly filled with helium. But that hasn't solved all their problems. Although helium is safer because it is less flammable, it is not as light as hydrogen. It takes more helium to lift the same amount of weight as hydrogen. And, being more scarce, it is harder to fill a blimp with helium.

Chapter 6
Floating on Air
The Aérotrain

Jean Bertin was a French inventor and aircraft engineer. He came up with an idea for a monorail train in 1965. It would hover over the track and move on a cushion of air. Without the friction from the track, it would be able to travel at very high speeds. Bertin called it the Aérotrain.

He built a test track and a scale model that could seat two people. It worked just like he had envisioned. The first model moved at 125 miles (201 km) per hour. After the addition of special engines, it moved at 214 miles (344 km) per hour.

More improvements followed on his second **prototype**. It carried six people and traveled at 262 miles (422 km) per hour.

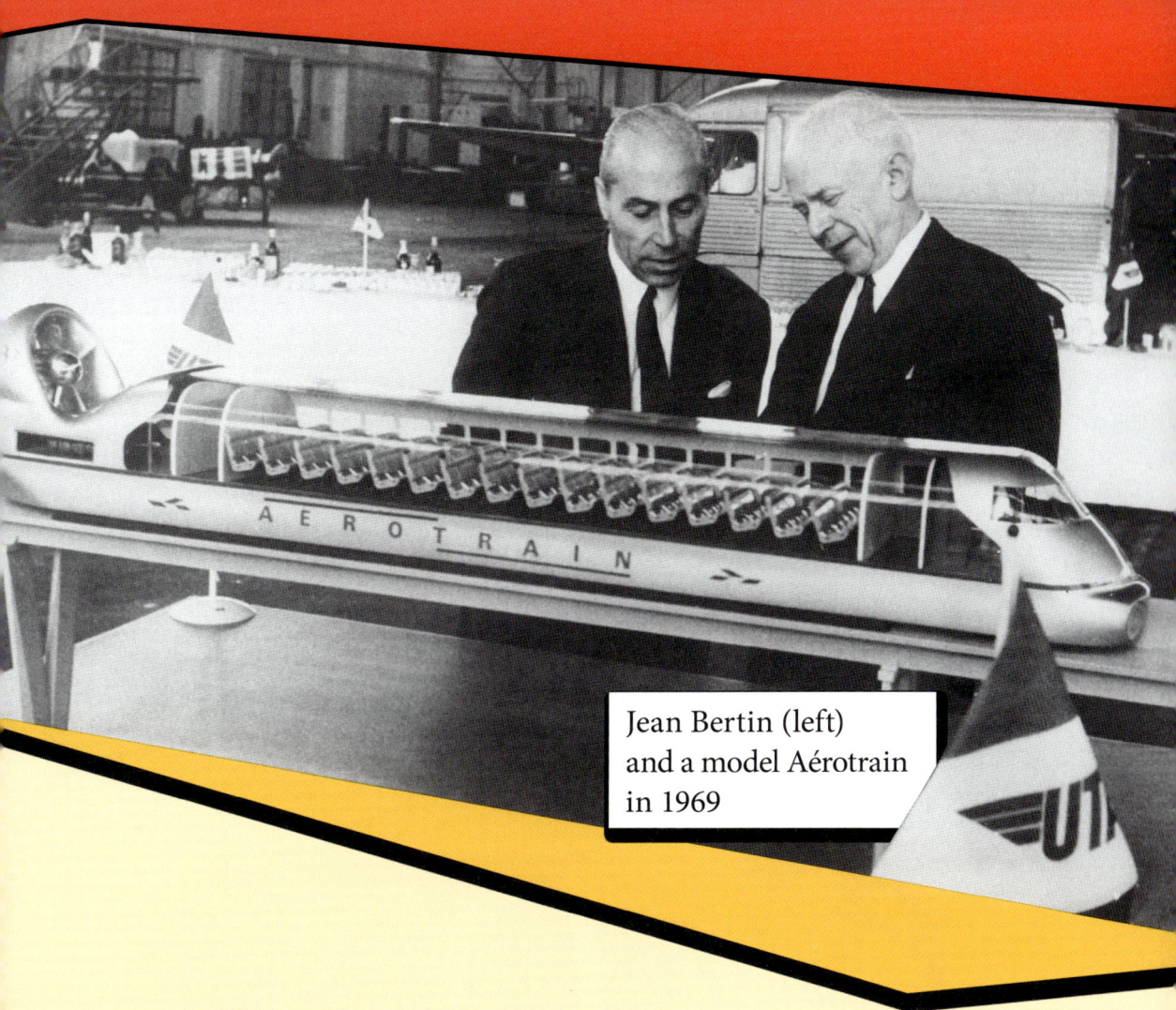

Jean Bertin (left) and a model Aérotrain in 1969

Magnetic Levitation

Most high-speed trains today are called maglev trains. Short for magnetic levitation, maglev trains are able to float above the tracks thanks to powerful electromagnets. Magnets underneath the car create a magnetic field and repel each other. This pushes the train up above the track. Metal set into the track is electrified. This creates another magnetic field that pushes and pulls the train forward.

All of Bertin's test runs were successful. He believed that his Aérotrains would be popular in the future. His final Aérotrain was built in 1969. It could carry 80 people.

FACT: The test track for Bertin's Aérotrain is still in place just outside of Paris, France.

The Aérotrain would have connected the French town of Pointoise to the city of Paris, a distance of 25 miles (40 km).

The French government saw Bertin's invention. Officials knew it worked well. But they didn't want it to be a success. Its existence meant the end of the railroad that was already in place in the country. That would be a lot of wasted taxpayer money.

French leaders made a big decision. They refused to give Bertin any more money to test his invention. Without the funding and support from the government, Bertin's invention stopped dead in its tracks.

Lessons Learned

Sometimes ideas can be good ones. Sometimes ideas can be great ones. But sometimes no matter how good or great they are, they don't go any further. Without money or support, it's difficult for an invention to be successful. If the product isn't available to the people, it's a failure.

CHAPTER 7

JET-SETTER THE CONCORDE

The Concorde was a turbojet **supersonic** airliner. It took its maiden flight in 1969. The plane flew at incredible speeds. It flew at **Mach** 2.04, which is about 1,565 miles (2,520 km) per hour. Regular passenger jetliners could travel at only about 540 miles (870 km) per hour.

EMPTY YOUR WALLETS

The Concorde may have been fast, but it was also extremely expensive to fly. It burned 100 tons of fuel traveling between New York and London. Today's Boeing 777 only uses 44 tons of fuel for the same trip.

Because of the high fuel prices, passenger tickets were equally as high. A round-trip ticket for a New York to London flight could cost as much as $17,000. Not many people could afford to pay for such expensive airfare. The Concorde really only flew the rich.

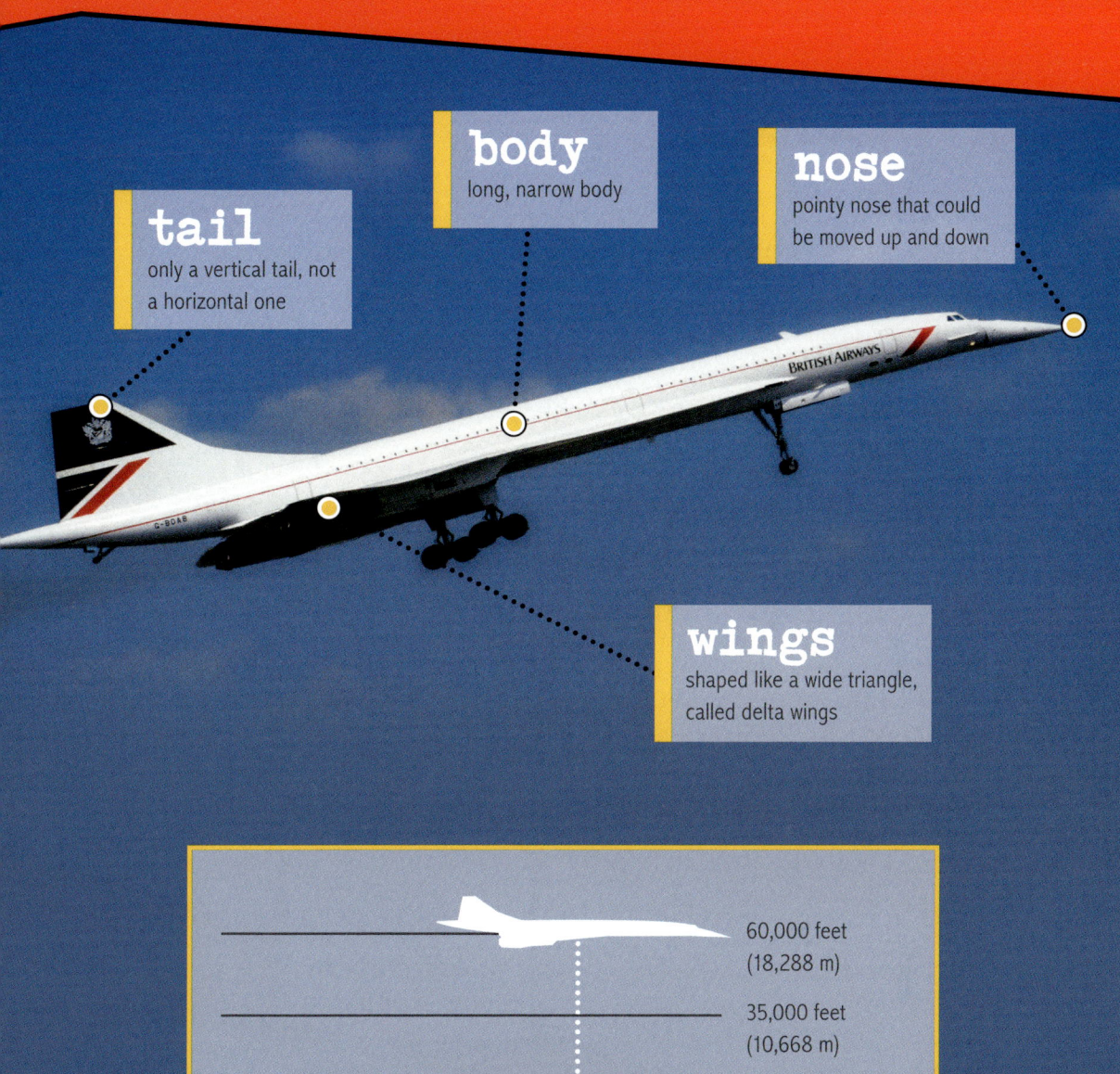

tail — only a vertical tail, not a horizontal one

body — long, narrow body

nose — pointy nose that could be moved up and down

wings — shaped like a wide triangle, called delta wings

60,000 feet (18,288 m)

35,000 feet (10,668 m)

The Concorde flew at 60,000 feet while regular jetliners fly at 35,000 feet.

FACT: It took a regular plane 17 hours to fly from London to Singapore. The Concorde could make it in seven hours.

PROBLEMS

There were also other problems with the aircraft. The plane's cabin was extremely narrow. It was only about 8 feet (2.4 m) wide and 6.4 feet (2 m) tall. Many people preferred flying on more spacious aircraft where they had room to move around.

The seats were small, rigid, and uncomfortable. Many said that it was clear that the plane was built for speed, not for comfort.

When the plane took off and landed, there was a loud **sonic boom**. Many countries didn't allow the Concorde in their airspace because of the noise it created. People were worried that supersonic travel could hurt Earth's atmosphere.

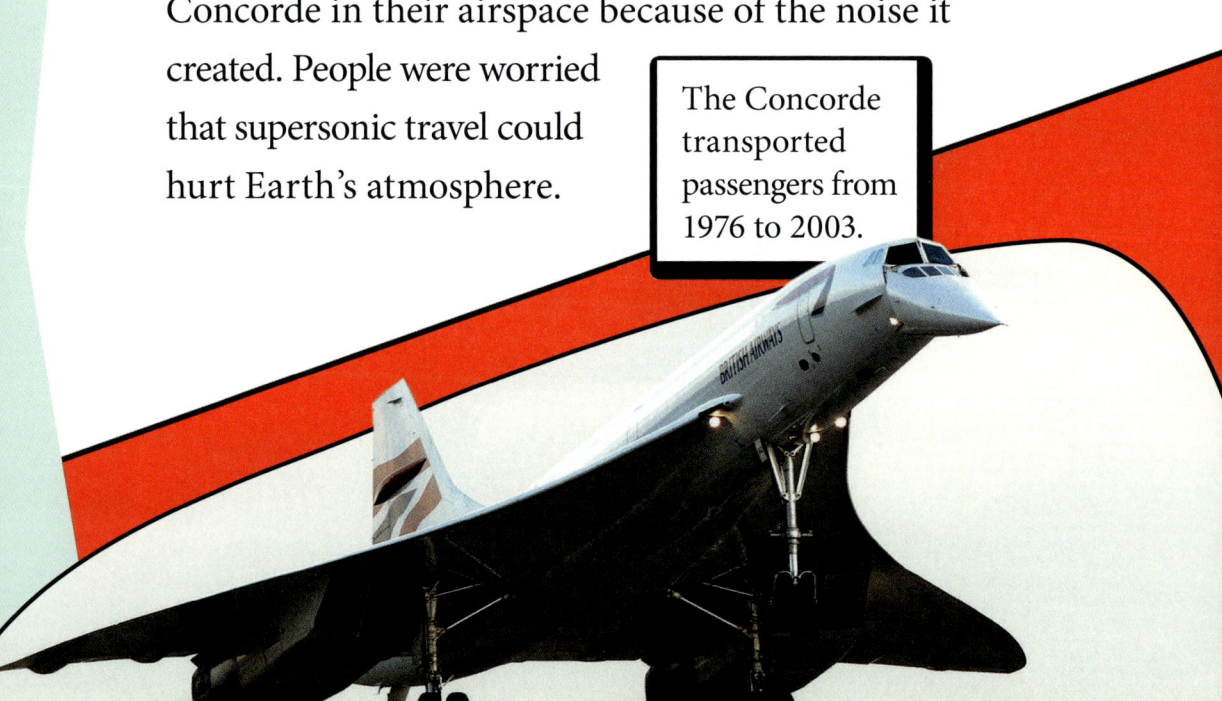

The Concorde transported passengers from 1976 to 2003.

THE END

In 2000, a Concorde crashed after takeoff in France. A piece of metal had punctured one of the tires. The damaged tire flung debris onto the plane's engines, and they caught on fire. Everyone on board died.

FACT: An international businessman named Fred Finn took a record number of Concorde flights—718 times.

The entire fleet of Concordes were inspected. They all needed to be updated, including adding bulletproof coverings to the fuel tanks and tougher tires. It cost the company about $21 million (£17 million). But things didn't end there. Additional accidents pushed the airlines to stop flying the Concorde. The Concorde made its final flight on October 24, 2003.

Lessons Learned

People still love the idea of supersonic travel. However, engineers need to find a less expensive way to operate supersonic jets, while ensuring each piece of the plane is properly protected. Also, comfort is important. The interior designs of any future supersonic craft would need to be more traveler friendly.

CHAPTER 8
LEMON IN THE SKY

THE FLYING PINTO

Who hasn't dreamed of a flying car? In 1973, one inventor made his dreams a reality when he built the AVE Mizar, or Flying Pinto. His name was Henry Smolinski.

Smolinski was an engineer who helped design jet engines and aircraft. He decided to start his own company with his friend, Hal Blake, in 1971.

Their plan for how their flying car would work included several steps. People would drive to the airport, get airplane wings attached to their cars, and then fly to their destinations. When they landed, they would detach the wings before driving away. The inventors dreamed that anyone and everyone could have a flying car.

The Flying Pinto's wings, tail fin, and rear engine were detachable. They could be operated from inside the car.

A Transportation Lemon

A Pinto is a small car that was built by the Ford Motor Company in the 1970s. This cheap, lightweight car had some flaws. If it was hit from behind, its fuel tanks might catch fire. In worst-case scenarios, the car would explode. Twenty-seven people died as a result of those fires. The Pinto was a lemon—a car with unfixable problems that occur over and over. *Time* magazine named this car one of the worst cars of all time in 2010.

Pintos were built between 1970 and 1980.

The AVE Mizar was going to be a villain's getaway car in a James Bond movie. After its failure, the movie makers had to find a different vehicle.

The Pinto was strapped to the wings of a small plane called a Cessna Skymaster. The steering wheel and pedals on the car were adapted so that the driver could control the flaps on the wings and tail of the plane. Once it was in the air, the flying car could move at 130 miles (209 km) per hour. The prototype was called the AVE Mizar. AVE stood for Advanced Vehicle Engineers, the name of Smolinski and Blake's company.

The first test flight took place in 1973. Just after takeoff, the pilot realized that part of the wing was no longer attached to the car. He landed in a nearby field. The flight lasted only a few minutes, but people were excited that it had worked at all. Smolinski had shown that the car could take off, fly, and then land.

The prototype was improved. Smolinski and Blake took it out for a test flight on September 11, 1973. Once again, the car was only in the air for a few moments. But this time, it didn't land safely in a field. It fell apart in midair. Pieces fell to the ground below. Smolinski and Blake were killed in the crash.

Lessons Learned

One of the main problems with this air car was that it was too heavy. The weight limited its flight time. The Mizar also failed because the wings were attached poorly to the car. Inspections of vehicles are very important because they can catch problems and prevent fatal accidents.

CHAPTER 9
BEEP BEEP
DICKMANNS'S SELF-DRIVING CAR

The idea of getting in a car and traveling to a destination while still being able to read, nap, or do other activities has been around for a while. In 1985, German engineer Ernst Dickmanns started working on a self-driving, or autonomous, car.

Dickmanns's van used a camera, computer, and sensors to navigate. By 1983, the van took its first drive on Germany's **autobahn**. It reached speeds of 56 miles (90 kilometers) per hour. It looked like his self-driving cars were the technology of the future.

But technology at the time was having a hard time keeping up. During this time, it could take a computer up to 10 minutes to analyze an image. There was no way a car could take that long while driving. Dickmanns figured that a driving car would need to analyze at least 10 images every second. How could he make that happen?

Ernst Dickmanns shows off the cameras mounted on his self-driving car.

The Man Behind the Car

Ernst Dickmanns was born in Germany in 1936. He studied aeronautics and aerospace, the technologies of traveling through the atmosphere around Earth and in space. His work led to the idea of driverless planes and helicopters.

Dickmanns programmed the computers to look at roads in the way that people see them. Instead of looking at everything, the computers would only look at things that were relevant to driving, such as road signs and lines. The van could also learn from its mistakes. The van drove hundreds of miles across Europe. Dickmanns hoped that eventually the computers could make their own driving decisions.

This sounded easier than it actually was. The van did all right on highways with other cars all driving in the same direction at similar speeds and in clearly

In the late 1990s, Dickmanns worked for the United States Army. In this job, he continued to work on self-driving car technology.

marked lanes. But regular roads were a challenge. Cars came from all directions. Sometimes cars in the distance covered road lines. Other times, the lines were faded or nonexistent. The van's computers didn't know what to do.

FACT: Experts predict that 10 to 30 percent of all cars will be fully self-driving by 2030.

Car manufacturers wanted immediate results. Dickmanns's research was expensive and too slow. They pulled their funding and the project was over.

Lessons Learned

Sometimes an idea is a good one, but technology isn't advanced enough to pull it off. Dickmanns's computer just couldn't process information fast enough to react in real time. But that doesn't mean the search for the self-driving car is over. Technology has advanced a lot since the 1980s. Today, many new cars help drivers park, let them know when an object gets too close, and even control the brakes or steering when the computer senses the driver is making a mistake.

CHAPTER 10
WATCH YOUR HEAD!

TRANSIT ELEVATED BUS

The huge country of China has a population to match its size. It also has major problems with traffic and air pollution. One of the country's challenges is how to get people from place to place efficiently, while also reducing its **carbon footprint**. China releases more pollution into the air than any other country in the world.

In 2010, the Transit Elevated Bus (TEB) tried to fix the pollution problem. Known as the "straddling bus," it straddled the roadway and allowed cars to drive underneath it.

Five cities signed on to be test sites. It was named one of the best inventions of 2010 by *Time* magazine. Investors contributed more than $500,000,000.

FACT: Burning fossil fuels, such as coal, natural gas, and crude oil sends harmful carbon dioxide emissions into Earth's atmosphere. This contributes to climate change, which can lead to many negative impacts on the planet.

A model showed future passengers how the Transit Elevated Bus could save space on the road.

The designers hoped that the TEB would help China's traffic problems in many ways. The TEB could:

- hold 300 passengers
- move down the tracks at 25 to 37 miles (40 to 60 km) per hour
- replace 40 conventional buses
- run partially on solar energy and save 860 tons of fuel
- prevent 2,640 tons of carbon **emissions** from entering the atmosphere

By 2016, two prototypes of the TEB were built and tested. They were constructed on a set of 984-foot (300-m)-long tracks that were set up on either side of a roadway. The TEB would move along the tracks while cars and other vehicles passed underneath. It was almost like the TEB was a moving bridge that could carry passengers.

The TEB sounded like a clever idea, but it ended up not working out. The TEB didn't really move fast enough to help out commuters. A car could drive

Building one TEB and 25 miles (40 km) of track would cost one-tenth as much as building a subway line.

on the same roadway at speeds twice as fast. Not all vehicles could safely pass underneath. Cars over 7 feet (2 m) were too tall.

The TEB was also too tall. At 15 feet (4.6 m) high, it couldn't pass underneath bridges on the roadway. It blocked drivers from seeing road lights and signs.

To make matters even worse, it was also too wide. It fit within two lanes of traffic. But if it had to move over for any reason, it crossed into additional road space. This could be extra dangerous if cars were driving under the TEB at the time.

Lessons Learned

Just because something solves some problems doesn't mean it won't create additional issues. There are many factors to think about, especially when dealing with moving vehicles. The TEB might have been successful if roads were straight and flat, and if cars traveled at the same pace and in the same lane the entire time.

DRIVING, FLYING, AND LAUNCHING THROUGH HISTORY

1813: George Stephenson builds the first steam-powered locomotive. He also engineered the first public railway, which opened in England in 1825.

1852: Henri Giffard builds the first powered airship, the dirigible.

1869: Construction on Beach's Pneumatic Transit begins.

1886: Karl Benz patents the first modern car, a three-wheeled, two-seated car powered by a gasoline engine.

1893: Speer's moving sidewalk debuts at Chicago's World's Fair.

1900: Count Ferdinand, Graf von Zeppelin, invents the first rigid airship.

October 1903: Samuel Langley tests his first full-sized Aerodrome.

December 1903: Orville and Wilbur Wright fly the first powered, heavier-than-air aircraft.

1912: The *Titanic* sets sail.

1937: The *Hindenburg* crashes.

1942: The first rocket to reach space is launched by German scientists.

1969: Jean Bertin builds the Aérotrain.

1969: Neil Armstrong and Buzz Aldrin become the first people to walk on the moon while Michael Collins orbits the moon in the command module.

1969: The first Concorde launches.

1973: Henry Smolinski takes his first test flight in his Flying Pinto.

1986: Ernst Dickmanns sends his self-driving car down the road.

2009: The Google Self-Driving Car Project begins. In 2016, it is renamed Waymo. Through 2018, the cars log more than 8 million miles (13 million kilometers).

2010: The Transit Elevated Bus is built to tackle air pollution in China.

GLOSSARY

aerodynamics (ayr-oh-dy-NA-miks)—the study of wind resistance

astronomer (uh-STRAH-nuh-muhr)—a scientist who studies stars, planets, and other objects in space

autobahn (AH-toh-bohn)— highways in Germany, Switzerland, and Austria, some with no speed limit

carbon footprint (KAHR-buhn FOOT-prihnt)—the amount of greenhouse gases, including carbon dioxide, emitted during a given period

elevated (EL-uh-vay-ted)—something that is lifted above the ground

emissions (ee-MI-shuhnz)—substances released into the air by an engine

flammable (FLA-muh-buhl)—likely to catch fire

grant (GRANT)—a gift such as land or money given for a particular purpose

hull (HUL)—the main body of a ship, which makes it float

mach (MAHK)—a unit of measurement for speeds faster than the speed of sound; Mach 2 is twice the speed of sound; the speed of sound is about 760 miles (1,220 km) per hour at sea level

novelty (NOV-uhl-tee)—something new, original, or unusual

pier (PIHR)—a platform that extends over a body of water

pneumatic (noo-MAT-ik)—operated by compressed air

prototype (pro-toh-TIPE)—the first version of an invention that tests an idea to see if it will work

rigid (RI-jihd)—stiff and inflexible

scale (SKALE)—to adjust a measurement according to a rate or standard

skeptic (SKEP-tik)—a person who questions things in which other people believe

sonic boom (SOH-nik BOOM)—a sound resembling an explosion that results from an aircraft traveling faster than the speed of sound

supersonic (soo-pur-SON-ik)—faster than the speed of sound

READ MORE

McCollum, Sean. *Fighting to Survive Airplane Crashes: Terrifying True Stories.* North Mankato, MN: Compass Point Books, 2020.

Durkin, Megan Ray. *What Would It Take to Make a Flying Car?* North Mankato, MN: Capstone Press, 2020.

Krajnik, Elizabeth. *Aboard the* Titanic. New York: Gareth Stevens Publishing, 2020.

INTERNET SITES

Fun Airplane Facts for Kids
http://www.sciencekids.co.nz/sciencefacts/vehicles/airplanes.html

Engineering for Kids
https://www.engineeringforkids.com/

History of Trains for Kids
https://www.dkfindout.com/us/transportation/history-trains/

Transportation Facts for Kids
https://easyscienceforkids.com/all-about-transportation/

INDEX

Aérotrain, 24–27
air pressure, 4, 7
AVE Mizar. *See* Flying Pinto

Beach, Alfred Ely, 4, 5, 6, 7
Beach's Pneumatic Transit System, 4–7
Bertin, Jean, 24, 25, 26, 27
Blake, Hal, 32, 34, 35
blimps, 21, 23

Cessna Skymaster, 34
Chicago's World's Fair, 8, 10
Concorde, 28–31
Count Ferdinand, Graf von Zeppelin, 20
crashes, 15, 16, 22, 31, 35

Dickmanns, Ernst, 36, 37, 38, 39

engines, 13, 14, 15
explosions, 22, 33

fires, 10, 22, 31
Flying Pinto, 32–35

Graf Zeppelin, 20, 21, 22

Hindenburg, 22, 23

Langley, Samuel, 12, 13, 14, 15

maglev trains, 25
models, 12, 13, 24, 25, 41
moving sidewalks, 8–11

Navy Pier, 8

prototypes, 24, 34, 35, 42

Samuel Langley's Aerodrome, 12–15
self-driving car, 36–39
Smithsonian Museum, 12
Smolinski, Henry, 32, 34, 35
Speer, Alfred, 8, 10, 11
subways, 6

Titanic, 16–19
trains, 4, 7, 11, 24, 25, 26, 27
Transit Elevated Bus (TEB), 40–43

Wright brothers, 14, 15
zeppelins, 20–23